Better Homes and Gardens®

# ANNUALS PERENNIALS AND BULBS

Excerpted from Better Homes and Gardens® *STEP-BY-STEP SUCCESSFUL GARDENING*

**BETTER HOMES AND GARDENS® BOOKS**

Editor: Gerald M. Knox
Art Director: Ernest Shelton
Managing Editor: David A. Kirchner
Editorial Project Managers: James D. Blume, Marsha Jahns,
   Rosanne Weber Mattson, Mary Helen Schiltz

Garden, Projects, and New Products Editor:
   Douglas A. Jimerson
Associate Editor: Jane Austin McKeon

Associate Art Directors: Linda Ford Vermie,
   Neoma Thomas, Randall Yontz
Assistant Art Directors: Lynda Haupert, Harijs Priekulis,
   Tom Wegner
Graphic Designers: Mary Schlueter Bendgen, Mike Burns,
   Brian Wignall
Art Production: Director: John Berg;
   Associate: Joe Heuer
   Office Manager: Michaela Lester

President, Book Group: Fred Stines
Vice President, General Manager: Jeramy Lanigan
Vice President, Retail Marketing: Jamie L. Martin
Vice President, Administrative Services: Rick Rundall

**BETTER HOMES AND GARDENS® MAGAZINE**
President, Magazine Group: James A. Autry
Vice President, Editorial Director: Doris Eby
Executive Director, Editorial Services: Duane L. Gregg

**ANNUALS, PERENNIALS, AND BULBS**
Editorial Project Manager: Rosanne Weber Mattson
Graphic Designer: Brian Wignall
Electronic Text Processor: Paula Forest

# CONTENTS

## ANNUALS     4

Annuals in the Landscape ................................. 4
Sowing Seeds Indoors ..................................... 8
Sowing Seeds Outdoors.................................... 10
Starting Annuals from
    Transplants........................................... 12
Annuals in Containers .................................... 14
Care and Maintenance..................................... 16

## PERENNIALS     18

Perennials in the
    Landscape............................................. 18
Planning a Perennial
    Border ............................................... 22
A Succession of Bloom..................................... 24
Gallery of Perennials...................................... 26
Care and Maintenance..................................... 30

## BULBS     32

Bulbs in the Landscape .................................... 32
Bulb Planting............................................. 36
Gallery of Bulbs.......................................... 38
Care and Maintenance .................................... 42
Forcing Bulbs ............................................ 44

## ZONE MAP     46

## INDEX     48

# ANNUALS IN THE LANDSCAPE

Large or small, formal or informal, bold or subdued—whatever your landscape style, annuals can fit pleasantly into the plan. While perennials and bulbs go in and out of bloom, annuals provide the flower garden with season-long color and continuity.

As you design your garden, keep in mind that bright, exciting colors make the garden appear smaller than it actually is. Cool tones, which are more soothing to the eye, will make your garden seem larger. The mixed spring border *below* pops with bright, warm tones of red, yellow, and orange.

If you like a vivid color scheme, try marigolds, salvia, snapdragons, or celo-sia. For subtler tones, select the blues and violets of pansies, ageratums, or lobelias for a cooler, more tranquil effect. In any flower combination, choose complementary hues for an eye-pleasing canvas of color.

The mixture of Shirley poppies, annual chrysanthemums, and California poppies at *right* gives an informal, country look to this suburban garden. Cosmos and spider flower, with an edging of sweet alyssum, would also look lovely. If you'd like a more formal look, stick with beds of one variety of annual. Good choices include geraniums, marigolds, and petunias. For contrast, add a silvery dusty-miller edging.

# ANNUALS IN THE LANDSCAPE

Flower beds should be geared to the existing climate and soil conditions. The garden at *right* includes statice, ice plant, daisies, portulaca, and California poppies, because these plants favor the dry soil found there. Sweet alyssum, zinnia, and vinca also do well in dry soil. Adding organic matter prior to planting helps conserve soil moisture in areas where water is scarce.

Cooler, moister annual beds are best planted with flowers such as browallia, lobelia, pansies, and salpiglossis. A mulch helps keep the soil cool and moist all season long.

When selecting annuals for your flower beds, remember that the most interesting combinations come from mixing plant sizes and shapes. For example, tall, spiked African marigolds look good behind bushy plants of cosmos, which taper down to mounds of dahlias or celosia. In the foreground, you can use ground-hugging gazania, annual phlox, dianthus, or verbena.

Flowers and foliage also offer a variety of sizes, shapes, and textures, and are effective when mixed. The daisy-like blossoms of gaillardia, spikes of salvia, and puffs of ageratum go well together. Foliage can be fine-textured, like the leaves on cosmos, or coarse, like those on the sunflower. Consider, too, the silver leaves of dusty-miller, the bronze of some begonias, the patterns of coleus, or the scalloping of nasturtium leaves.

Your garden can have color even if it's shaded by a variety of trees and buildings. A bed of impatiens (*right*) grows happily in subdued light. Try low-growing types like Super Elfins, Minis, or Accents; medium-size Cinderella or Novette; or tall Blitz.

Another good choice for shaded areas is the wax (fibrous) begonia. In climates where high heat and humidity exist, use bronze-leaved wax begonias. Coleus also does well in dark areas. All three of these shade-lovers need a minimum of maintenance after planting—just water them regularly.

Let your annuals play the roles for which they are best suited. Leading ladies for cool-climate container plants include pansies, dianthus, and Martha Washington geraniums (*right*). If you'd like to fill a planter with petunias, one of the large-flowered grandiflora types would be best. But if you want a petunia for a mass effect in a flower bed, select a multiflora type, which is more weather- and disease-resistant, and will produce a greater number of flowers.

If you enjoy bringing the beauty of your garden indoors, plant annuals that make good cut flowers, including aster, celosia, cosmos, dahlia, zinnia, stock, snapdragon, salvia, marigold, and poppy. Select baby's-breath, strawflower, statice, or other everlastings if you plan to dry flowers.

# SOWING SEEDS INDOORS

Why start plants from seeds indoors? Along with providing you with a pleasant late-winter project, it lets you plant certain flower seeds that are too small to be grown outdoors or take such a long time to bloom that they need a head start. Annuals that will grow better if you start them indoors include ageratum, begonia, coleus, dianthus, geranium, impatiens, lobelia, African marigold, pansy, petunia, salpiglòssis, salvia, snapdragon, or verbena.

## PLANTING

■ Timing is important. Although most annuals should be started indoors 6 to 8 weeks before planting outdoors, the tiny seeds of begonia, coleus, dianthus, geranium, impatiens, lobelia, pansy, petunia, salvia, and verbena should be started 10 to 12 weeks ahead.

To sow seeds indoors, choose an appropriate container. You can purchase plastic or peat flats, or make your own from clean, 3-inch-deep containers with drainage holes in the bottom. Fill the container with a mixture of peat moss and perlite or vermiculite, which you can combine yourself or buy ready-mixed. This lightweight potting media is more sterile than regular garden soil, and will help prevent damping-off disease, which can kill or damage young seedlings. An application of benomyl solution will further protect your seedlings from disease.

Fill the container to within ¼ inch of the top with premoistened media. Sow seeds evenly and thinly over the top. Cover seeds with media only as deep as their thickness; don't cover fine seeds at all. Label the container and place it in a plastic bag, tied tightly to retain moisture. Keep in indirect sunlight.

## KEEPING THEM GROWING

■ When seeds have germinated, remove the plastic bag and place seedlings in a sunny location. To avoid uprooting the plants, water from the bottom. Once the plants are showing growth, add fertilizer to the water.

The first growth will be food-storing parts called cotyledons. After two sets of true leaves have developed, transplant seedlings into their own pots.

## TRANSPLANTING

■ Just before transplanting outside, harden off your seedlings (get them accustomed to the outdoors). Place them outside in a protected spot (a cold frame or screened porch is ideal) for a few hours a day, increasing the time every day. As soon as the garden soil dries, plant as you would purchased bedding plants, described on page 12.

When transplanting seedlings, handle them only by the leaves. The plant can grow another leaf if damaged, but it can't grow another stem.

# SOWING SEEDS OUTDOORS

It's more economical to sow seeds outdoors than to plant purchased bedding plants, and seed racks give you a wider selection of varieties to choose from. Seeds won't give you instant results, however, and your success will be more dependent on Mother Nature. Whichever method you use, select varieties carefully by studying catalogs and seed packets. Different varieties offer different colors, heights, and resistance to weather, insects, and disease.

Timing is critical for sowing seeds outdoors. Some annuals are called "cool-season" types, and may be sown as early in spring as the soil can be worked. Wait to plant "warm-season" annuals until the chance of frost is past.

While some smaller annual seeds must be started indoors, the following can be started from seed sown directly in the garden:

- African daisy*
- Amaranthus
- Aster
- Calendula*
- California poppy*
- Candytuft
- Cape daisy
- Carnation
- Celosia
- Cleome
- Coreopsis
- Cornflower
- Cosmos
- Dahlia
- Dusty-miller
- Gaillardia
- Kochia
- Larkspur*
- Marigold
- Nasturtium
- Nemesia*
- Nierembergia
- Nigella*
- Phlox*
- Portulaca
- Scabiosa
- Stocks*
- Sweet alyssum*
- Sweet pea*
- Tithonia
- Zinnia

*Cool-season annual

Avoid the temptation to work soil too early. Wet soil will harden when it dries, preventing good root growth. To test for readiness, take a handful of soil and squeeze it; if it stays together, the soil is too wet for you to work. Wait a few days and try the test again.

When it's time to sow your seeds, pay particular attention to planting depth. If seeds are planted too shallow, they will dry out and not germinate. But if seeds are planted too deep, the soil may be too cold, may lack oxygen, or may present too much of a barrier for seeds to push through. A good rule is to plant seeds as deep as they are thick.

Some fine seeds, usually grown indoors, can be sown outdoors with the help of seed pellets or seed tapes, which you cut and lay on the ground.

Space most annuals a distance apart that is half of their mature height. Read seed packets for recommendations. Follow the spacing guidelines given below in inches for these annuals:

- African daisy 10–12
- Ageratum 6–8
- Aster 12–15
- Begonia 7–9
- Cleome 12–24
- Coleus 10–18
- Marigold 6–15
- Nasturtium 8–12
- Oriental pepper 6–8
- Pansy 4–6
- Petunia 12–14
- Salvia 6–8
- Snapdragon 6–8
- Sweet alyssum 6
- Sweet pea 10–12
- Zinnia 6–12

**1** Good soil preparation is the key to a thriving, colorful annual garden. If you have a tiller, you can eliminate hand-spading and till the garden to a depth of 8 to 10 inches. Run the tiller across the first rows to break up soil even more. This method works well when starting a new flower bed.

**3** Lay pieces of cord or clothesline on the ground to outline a design within the flower bed. Sow seeds evenly over the ground; cover slightly with soil. Keep moist by watering with a gentle spray from a sprinkler or hose, until strong growth appears.

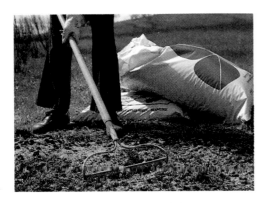

**2** Prepare the seedbed by incorporating organic material such as peat moss, compost, or manure; perlite or vermiculite for added porosity; and fertilizer. Work material in, apply water, and rake smooth; seeds will not germinate and grow in compacted, lumpy, or dry soil.

**4** After the seedlings have developed two to three sets of leaves, you'll need to thin them. Carefully remove seedlings so that you don't disturb the others. Leave space between plants; as outlined on the chart on the previous page. After thinning, remove the cords you used to define the area.

**5** Thinning allows your plants to grow to their ultimate size and shape. In a short time, your garden will look like the warm array of colors from the cosmos, zinnias, and marigolds pictured *above*.

If you remove the thinnings carefully, you can transplant them to another part of the garden or give them to friends. Label each plant so you'll remember what it is. To help you make choices for next season, record the varieties you've planted and how well they've performed for you.

# STARTING ANNUALS FROM TRANSPLANTS

Bedding plants are right for you if you want an instant garden of beautiful blooms, or if you don't have the time, space, or inclination to start your own annuals from seed. Started flats and packs of almost any type of flowering annual can be purchased at local garden centers. Most of these plants should be planted after the last frost in your area. These transplants can give you a jump on summer color and transform your flower beds almost overnight from dull to sensational.

You'll get a lot of enjoyment from your annual investment in bedding plants. Professionally grown, they will be larger and easier to handle, will give you at least an extra month of color, and will be better established before mid-summer's heat and drought have a chance to wilt and kill them.

**1** When you shop for bedding plants, look for compact, bright green, healthy plants. The label will tell you about variety, color, and height. Don't reject those that aren't in bloom; all-green plants often do better in the long run.

**2** If you can't plant right away, keep your new flowers moist. Remove the plants from the pack by holding them with one hand while inverting the pack. If they don't fall out easily, tap the bottom with a trowel.

**3** If the plants are not in individual cells, separate them gently by hand or with a knife just before planting; don't allow roots to dry out. Soil in the planting bed should be tilled, enriched, and watered before planting.

**4** If roots seem compacted, loosen them gently before planting. Dig a hole slightly larger than the root ball, and set the plant in place at the same level it grew before. Firm soil around the roots.

**5** Water well right after planting; water frequently until plants become established and new growth has started. Once that happens, plants fill in quickly. The photo at *right* was taken six weeks after the one *above*.

# ANNUALS IN CONTAINERS

If you don't have much yard space, consider filling containers to overflowing with annual flowers. Instant color from these flowers can have a dramatic impact on your deck or patio.

Container gardening has many advantages, including effectiveness and ease. Because there are no planting beds to prepare, you save time and energy. Even if ground space is at a premium in your yard, color can abound from containers set on patios, steps, paths, decks, and balconies. Containers can be put anywhere and moved about as your mood changes. If something doesn't look quite right, you can take it away, spruce it up, and bring it back.

## TYPES OF CONTAINERS
■ In addition to traditional flowerpots, a wide variety of containers is available: barrels, tubs, boxes, baskets, urns, plastic pipe, tree stumps, and even bags of potting soil.

Almost any container will do, as long as it has good drainage. Several holes in the bottom are a must to keep roots from getting waterlogged. If you want to use a decorative container with a solid bottom, place your plants in a draining-type pot that can sit inside the decorative one. A layer of gravel in the bottom of the outer pot will help prevent overwatering.

## PLANTING AND CARING
■ Use a soilless media of sphagnum peat moss (or other organic matter) with perlite or vermiculite in a 50/50 ratio. Adding sharp sand to the mix will help keep small containers from toppling over in windy spots.

Because you'll want instant effect, plant containers with purchased bedding plants or plants you started indoors, rather than with seed. Plant tightly for massed beauty.

Plants grown in containers need to be watered often because they dry out faster than they do in the ground. Every week or two while watering, add a soluble fertilizer at half or quarter strength to stimulate growth and constant flowering. To keep growth uniform, rotate the containers weekly if sunlight hits them unevenly. Pick faded blooms.

Plant pots with compact annuals that produce nonstop color, such as petunias, marigolds, pinks, sweet alyssum, impatiens, or geraniums (*left*). A tall plant, such as dracaena, will look good centered in a large pot, with ivy geraniums cascading over the rim. For best effect, keep everything in proportion.

# CARE AND MAINTENANCE

If a flower garden full of annual blooms is your goal, you must begin your care and maintenance program with good soil preparation and carefully organized planting. After that, you and Mother Nature will work together to produce a garden spot covered with color and life from spring to fall.

## FERTILIZING

■ Because annuals bloom for only one season, they can usually get by without being fed. Some annuals, including nasturtium, cleome, and portulaca, require no supplementary nourishment. Others, however, will perform better if they occasionally receive food in addition to their regular watering. For those that benefit from fertilizing, mix a balanced 5-10-5 food into the soil prior to planting. To keep annuals in top shape, feed them with a water-soluble fertilizer once a month to produce even growth and maximum flowering.

## WATERING

■ Deep, infrequent watering will promote better root growth than frequent, light applications. Any of the methods outlined on page 10 will work fine for annuals. If you plan to cut flowers for indoor bouquets, avoid overhead watering, which can damage the blossoms. Where hot, dry weather prevails, choose a drought-resistant annual, such as portulaca, four-o'clock, celosia, cosmos, sunflower, or zinnia.

## MULCHING

■ Mulch helps annuals grow by reducing weeds and conserving soil moisture. It also adds a clean, neat look to your flower bed. Apply a 3- to 4-inch layer of mulch around plants in the spring after your annuals are established. At the end of the season, spade organic mulches into the soil for a fertile planting bed the following year.

## STAKING

■ Top-heavy or tall annuals will need to be staked to keep them from bending and breaking. Use a sturdy stake, tying it loosely to the plant with cord or a twist tie. Tying too tightly can pinch or damage the stem.

## PRIMPING

■ Keep your garden neat by pulling weeds, removing faded flowers and discolored leaves, and pruning and trimming. Some annuals, such as petunias, may need to be cut back after their first flush of bloom to encourage a greater second bloom. This gardening chore will soon become a job of the past, however, because today's improved hybrids offer more bloom-power than their ancestors did.

After frost has blackened the tops of your annual garden in the fall, you can pull the plants or leave them to be incorporated into the soil next spring. Add to the compost pile any disease-free plants you pull.

## PEST CONTROL

■ Most annuals are rarely bothered by insects or diseases. Zinnias, however, are susceptible to mildew. You can control this problem by planting zinnias in open areas with good air circulation, and by avoiding overhead watering systems that get the foliage wet.

Many annual flowers, such as the marigold *above,* should be removed as they fade. This simple procedure, called deadheading, ensures maximum and continuous blooming all summer. Clip or snap off dead flowers.

Petunias can get leggy. To keep them compact and to induce more blooming, pinch them back by removing stems at leaf joinings. You'll also encourage growth by regularly cutting flowers for indoor bouquets.

1 You can multiply some annuals, such as the coleus *above,* by taking cuttings and rooting them. For best results, clip a stem about 4 inches long with at least 4 leaves. Remove the lowest 2 leaves, and apply a rooting hormone to the bottom.

2 Insert the cutting into a growing media of premoistened sphagnum peat moss and/or sand. Place the pot in a plastic bag and set it in an area with good light, but not direct sun. In about 10 days, check for rooting by gently pulling on the cutting.

3 When cuttings have rooted, remove them from the rooting media and transplant them to containers or to the garden, depending on the time of year. Other annuals that can be grown from cuttings include impatiens, geraniums, and begonias.

Many annuals, such as sweet alyssum, lobelia, and petunia (*above*), may get too bushy and encroach on other flowers. Use hedge clippers or shears to keep them in check. They'll resume blooming soon after trimming.

Make your garden easy to maintain by selecting the proper plant for your climate. For example, pansies (*above*), nemesia, baby-blue-eyes, and salpiglossis love cool weather, making them poorly suited for hot, dry climates.

Drought-tolerant plants, such as the portulaca (*above*), vinca, dusty-miller, geranium, and gazania, thrive where summers are hot and dry. Plant these annuals in a sunny garden location that has well-drained soil.

# PERENNIALS IN THE LANDSCAPE

Large or small, formal or informal, high- or low-maintenance, no garden is complete without a selection of perennials to lead it through the gardening season. Year after year, perennials offer an everchanging framework of color, filling borders with lovely flowers and a variety of foliage textures and shades of green. Unlike annuals, perennials don't require the time and expense of yearly replanting. Most will grow and bloom for many years without a lot of pampering. This sense of permanence adds continuity to the garden.

Whatever your soil and climatic conditions, you can find perennials in a wide selection of sizes, shapes, and colors to fulfill them. Perennials such as (front to back) Gold Drop rudbeckia, phlox, bee-balm, bellflower, cimicifuga, and ligularia pack the sunny border *below* with color in late summer.

Use perennials to take advantage of nooks and crannies you may have previously overlooked. A little ingenuity turned the thin strips of soil on either side of the front walk at *right* into a festival of flowers. Columbine, daylily, and iris mix with annuals like geranium, petunia, portulaca, zinnia, alyssum, and dwarf marigold to fill both beds to overflowing. Early in the spring, a variety of bulbs can fill the same beds for many months of color.

# PERENNIALS IN THE LANDSCAPE

Careful planning will reward you with a mixed perennial border that is abloom from spring to frost. Because most plants blossom for just a few weeks, you must plant a variety of perennials that bloom at successive intervals. To have constant bloom, assign each perennial to a spot where it will provide color at a specific period during the season.

Make your border at least 4 to 6 feet deep, and plant perennials so they're tapered in height. If the border is backed by a wall or fence, plant tall varieties in back and low growers in front. To enjoy an island bed from all sides, plant taller perennials in the center of the bed and have shorter plants radiate out to the edges. Group three or more of one variety and color in drifts for best visual impact.

In early summer, the garden *below* comes alive with spikes of foxglove in back, masses of peonies, columbine, and iris in the middle, and dianthus in front. Throughout the summer, other perennials will take over, such as phlox, lythrum, liatris, shasta daisy, and aster.

Combine perennials that bloom at different times to ensure a succession of color throughout the season. To make planning easier, the mixed flower garden at *right* is divided into smaller, easy-to-manage sections. In spring, bloom comes from columbine, forget-me-not, bleeding-heart, peony, iris, coralbell, and Virginia bluebell. Joining these perennials in summer are gaillardia, baptisia, hollyhock, delphinium, phlox, shasta daisy, astilbe, daylily, lupine, pinks, yarrow, and hardy lily. Late summer brings a grand finale of hardy asters and chrysanthemums.

Choose a color scheme for your border, too. For bright splashy colors, use a lot of reds, bright yellows, blues, and purples. A softer look can be made with pinks, blues, pale yellows, and white.

Many perennials will perform brightly without sunshine. In the shady border at *right,* sedum, astilbe, Siberian iris, rudbeckia, *Lobelia splendens,* and *Sanguisorba canadensis* grow in front of the tall Rocket ligularia. Other perennials that are made for the shade are bleeding-heart, hosta, fern, and columbine.

Nature's woodlands also provide us with a large family of flowers that bloom without the sun. Some favorite shade-loving wildflowers are bloodroot, dog-tooth violet, dutchman's-breeches, wild geranium, mayapple, jacob's-ladder, wild ginger, hepatica, jack-in-the-pulpit, sweet william, spring beauty, solomon's-seal, and trillium. To leave natural areas undisturbed, buy wildflower transplants or seeds from a local or mail-order nursery.

# PLANNING A PERENNIAL BORDER

There's more to perennial gardening than filling a border with pretty flowers. A prizewinning perennial border is one that gets its natural look from careful planning on the part of the gardener. When perennials are combined attractively in an informal design, each one gets a turn to be the spotlighted star of an ongoing floral show.

## COLOR

■ Color can be the framework of your garden design, providing accent, balance, repetition, and excitement. When combining perennials, choose a color scheme for each season, using one main color as a backbone: for example, yellow for spring, pink for early summer, blue for midsummer, and gold for fall. Blues and violets are cooler colors, and will make the garden appear larger; bolder reds, oranges, and yellows will add warmth to the design.

Select a few plants in each chosen color range, then sprinkle in a few secondary perennials in complementary colors. To avoid a checkerboard effect with small isolated spots of color, plant each perennial en masse and repeat throughout the border. For contrast, put similar or opposite colors near the massed colors. With orange daylilies, for example, use yellow coreopsis or clear blue anchusa.

## SHAPE AND TEXTURE

■ Variety in form and foliage adds spice to a garden. Use a mixture of mat and cushion plants, medium- and large-size mounded plants, and plants with spiked blossoms. Foliage types that you can choose from include coarse or soft, lance-shape or rounded, and flat or glossy. Base your final selections on a variety of plant heights, so that plants of all sizes appear in the garden design.

## STYLE

■ Formal or informal? This will be determined by your taste and the style of your home. Formal gardens are symmetrical; the more popular informal gardens are amorphous and most effective when laid out in curved drifts.

If you're new at perennial garden design, visit other gardens and note what blooms at various times, which plants create appealing combinations and contrasts, and which textures and colors can be integrated into your design.

## EARLY SUMMER

■ The ultimate challenge to any perennial gardener is to design a border with color and interest all summer. Any planning you do before planting will help eliminate the need to make changes later. The garden at *right* begins the summer with blooms from lythrum, daylily, black-eyed susan, gaillardia, and lily. Other perennials that bloom in early summer are gas plant, shasta daisy, thermopsis, and Canterbury-bells. All-season color in front comes from annuals, such as petunia, marigold, ageratum, zinnia, and salvia.

Before selecting plants, make note of the amount of sun the border will receive. The plants listed above are sun worshipers. Choose others if your garden will be shaded.

## MIDSUMMER

■ In midsummer, clumps of white and pink phlox, blue and purple delphinium, liatris, and veronica join the parade of perennial color. Other excellent profuse bloomers include balloon flower, scabiosa, lavender, cupid's-dart, butterfly weed, marguerite, snakeroot, globe thistle, hosta, coralbells, and bee-balm. Black-eyed susan, coreopsis, and blanketflower continue to flower from earlier in the summer.

Check the hardiness of the plants you have selected for your border and make sure they will survive the rigors of your winters. Draw the plan out to scale on graph paper to know how many plants to buy and how close together to plant them. Determine spacing between the plants by their size at maturity.

## LATE SUMMER

■ Late summer announces the arrival of chrysanthemums. Other perennials that offer autumn bloom include sedum, aster, goldenrod, helianthus, hardy ageratum, turtlehead, and physostegia.

Soil is an important element to consider when designing your perennial garden. Although you can and should improve garden soil before planting, some soil conditions will limit your planting choices. An always-moist soil, for example, won't provide a healthy home for perennials that require a well-drained soil. Fortunately, a number of perennials, including bergenia, filipendula, the cardinal flower, lysimachia, lythrum, forget-me-not, globe flower, and Japanese and Siberian iris, prefer to have their feet wet.

# A SUCCESSION OF BLOOM

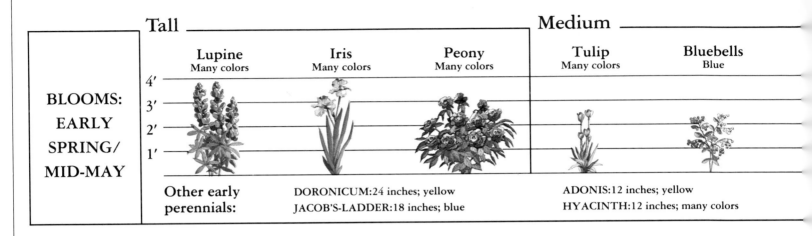

**Tall** —————————————————————————— **Medium** ———————

| | Lupine<br>Many colors | Iris<br>Many colors | Peony<br>Many colors | Tulip<br>Many colors | Bluebells<br>Blue |
|---|---|---|---|---|---|

BLOOMS:
EARLY
SPRING/
MID-MAY

4'
3'
2'
1'

**Other early perennials:** DORONICUM:24 inches; yellow ADONIS:12 inches; yellow
JACOB'S-LADDER:18 inches; blue HYACINTH:12 inches; many colors

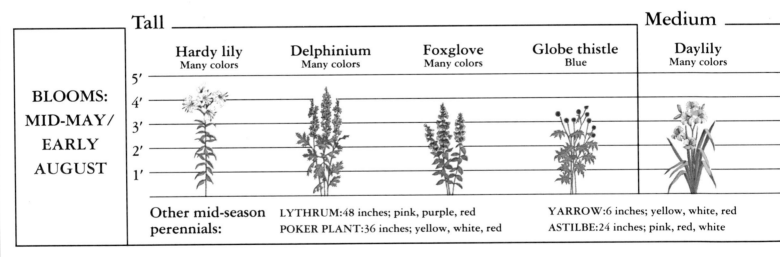

**Tall** —————————————————————————— **Medium** ———————

| | Hardy lily<br>Many colors | Delphinium<br>Many colors | Foxglove<br>Many colors | Globe thistle<br>Blue | Daylily<br>Many colors |
|---|---|---|---|---|---|

BLOOMS:
MID-MAY/
EARLY
AUGUST

5'
4'
3'
2'
1'

**Other mid-season perennials:** LYTHRUM:48 inches; pink, purple, red YARROW:6 inches; yellow, white, red
POKER PLANT:36 inches; yellow, white, red ASTILBE:24 inches; pink, red, white

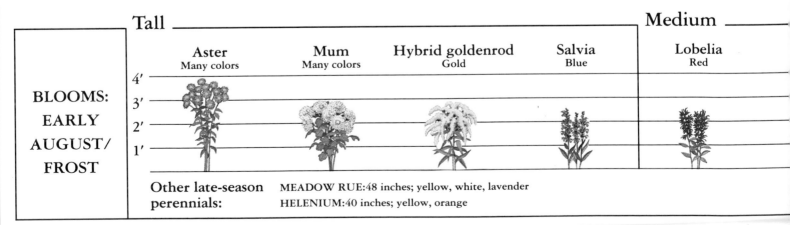

**Tall** —————————————————————————— **Medium** ———————

| | Aster<br>Many colors | Mum<br>Many colors | Hybrid goldenrod<br>Gold | Salvia<br>Blue | Lobelia<br>Red |
|---|---|---|---|---|---|

BLOOMS:
EARLY
AUGUST/
FROST

4'
3'
2'
1'

**Other late-season perennials:** MEADOW RUE:48 inches; yellow, white, lavender
HELENIUM:40 inches; yellow, orange

## Low

| Narcissus<br>Many colors | Bleeding-heart<br>Pink | Golden alyssum<br>Gold | Primrose<br>Many colors | Moss phlox<br>Many colors | Viola<br>Many colors |
|---|---|---|---|---|---|

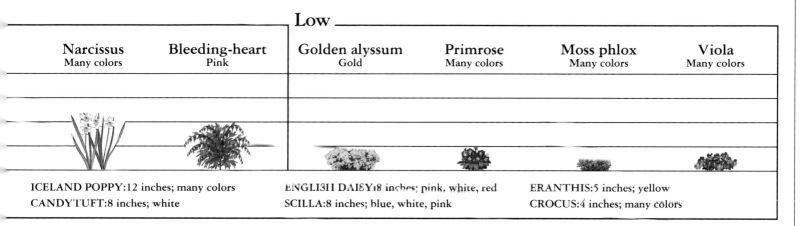

ICELAND POPPY:12 inches; many colors　　　　ENGLISH DAISY:18 inches; pink, white, red　　　　ERANTHIS:5 inches; yellow
CANDYTUFT:8 inches; white　　　　SCILLA:8 inches; blue, white, pink　　　　CROCUS:4 inches; many colors

## Low

| Baby's-breath<br>White, pink | Phlox<br>Many colors | Oriental poppy<br>Many colors | Shasta daisy<br>White | Lamb's-ears<br>Many colors | Sweet william<br>Many colors | Thrift<br>Rose, white |
|---|---|---|---|---|---|---|

COLUMBINE:24 inches; many colors　　　　CORALBELLS:18 inches; white, pink, red　　　　VERONICA:18 inches; blue, white, pink
LAVENDER:24 inches; lavender, blue　　　　COREOPSIS:18 inches; yellow　　　　PAINTED DAISY:24 inches; white, pink, red

## Low

| Coneflower<br>Yellow-orange | Hardy ageratum<br>Blue | Balloon flower<br>Blue, pink, white | Artemisia<br>Silver | Leadwort<br>Blue | Sedum<br>Many colors |
|---|---|---|---|---|---|

LIATRIS:48 inches; white, rose, purple　　　　HELIANTHUS:36 inches; yellow　　　　PHYSOSTEGIA:30 inches; white, pink
MONKSHOOD:40 inches; many colors　　　　FALL DAYLILIES:36 inches; many colors

25

# GALLERY OF PERENNIALS

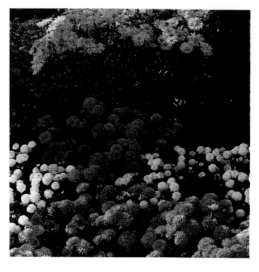

### ASTILBE hybrids
*Astilbe x arendsi*

Astilbe are attractive perennials for the shady garden border. Flowers produced in early to midsummer are feathery, pyramidal spikes in pink, white, red, or salmon. The foliage, with its finely cut, roselike leaves, is attractive even when the plant is not in bloom.
**SOIL:** Prefers moist soil, but does well in dry spots also.
**LIGHT:** Partial sun to heavy shade. For best growth, give higher light.
**HARDINESS:** Zone 6
**COMMENTS:** There are many good hybrid varieties. Fanal, Peach Blossom, Deutschland, Rheinland, and Superba are the best known.

Start plants in early spring from seed or by division. For best growth, keep plants well watered and fed. A two- to three-inch layer of mulch around the plant will keep roots cool and moist.

### CANDYTUFT
*Iberis sempervirens*

Candytuft is an excellent choice for the rock garden, borders, or edgings, because it grows only 8 to 12 inches tall. It produces tiny, white flowers in flat umbels or clusters in mid- to late spring. Foliage is evergreen, with long, narrow, shiny leaves that lie in a whorl around the stem.
**SOIL:** Rich, well drained
**LIGHT:** Full sun
**HARDINESS:** Zone 3
**COMMENTS:** The most popular varieties include: Little Gem, Snowflake, Purity, Autumn Snow, and Pygmy. The variety Autumn Snow is unique, because it blooms in both spring and fall.

After candytuft blooms, cut it back with a hedge cutter. This will keep it compact and ensure maximum flowering the following year. Candytuft grows easily from cuttings or seeds.

### CHRYSANTHEMUM
*Chrysanthemum* species and hybrids

Chrysanthemums are the crowning glory of the fall garden with all sizes of flowers in every color but true blue. Flower shapes include single, semidouble, anemone, pompon, incurve, reflexed, spoon, quill, or spider. The height of mums varies from low-growing cushion types to football mums several feet tall.
**SOIL:** Rich, well drained, heavily fed, and well watered
**LIGHT:** Full sun
**HARDINESS:** Zone 5
**COMMENTS:** To produce full flower heads, pinch mums from early spring to mid-July. There are hundreds of varieties that are excellent in the garden or in containers. Start new plants from seeds, root divisions, and stem cuttings. Or buy started plants in midsummer.

Shasta and painted daisies are relatives of the chrysanthemum. They start blooming earlier in the season.

## COREOPSIS (tickseed)
*Coreopsis* species

One of the most dependable and longest-blooming perennials is the coreopsis. Flowers, which appear from June until frost, are yellow, daisylike, and either single or double. The plant itself grows 24 to 30 inches tall and is relatively care-free. Some leaves are large and solid; some of them are lobed. The threadleaf coreopsis (*C. verticillata*) has very fine foliage.

**SOIL:** Any type
**LIGHT:** Full sun
**HARDINESS:** Zone 6
**COMMENTS:** To keep coreopsis at its peak of bloom, keep cutting away the flowers after they fade. If you enjoy cut flowers for the house, coreopsis is an excellent choice for your cutting garden. To propagate coreopsis, grow them from seed or divisions, lifted and replanted in either fall or spring.

## DAYLILY
*Hemerocallis* species and varieties

From the Greek word, meaning "beautiful for a day," the hemerocallis or daylily is one of the best plants for the perennial border or for planting along roadsides or on slopes. Their tight root systems make them good for erosion control. Lilylike flowers bloom in every color except true blue and pure white, on plants that can range from 18 to 36 inches tall. Swordlike leaves are relatively free from problems.

**SOIL:** Any type soil. Water needed only during droughts.
**LIGHT:** Full sun or part shade
**HARDINESS:** Zone 5
**COMMENTS:** Daylilies are grown for their lovely flowers, which have been greatly improved by breeding. Tens of thousands of varieties are now available. Although each flower lasts for only a day, the plants will be in flower for weeks. By combining varieties, you'll have color for months.

## DELPHINIUM
*Delphinium* species and hybrids

Dramatic is the best word to describe delphiniums. Although there are some dwarf varieties available, most reach 4 to 6 feet tall. Borne on long spikes, blooms appear in early summer and again in fall. True blue and purple are the most-recognized colors.

**SOIL:** Deep, rich, and light, with a pH of neutral or slightly alkaline. Soil should also be well drained, to prevent crown rot, and very fertile. Water well at all times.
**LIGHT:** Full sun
**HARDINESS:** Zone 3
**COMMENTS:** Delphiniums prefer a cool, moist climate, so they are difficult to grow in hot and dry areas. They are short-lived plants, and will need to be replaced every few years. Because they grow tall, they must be staked. When choosing varieties, look at the Pacific Giant and Connecticut Yankee hybrids for good performance.

# GALLERY OF PERENNIALS

## HOSTA (plantain lily, funkia)
*Hosta* species

Although the hosta does flower, it is primarily known as a foliage plant for beds, borders, or as a ground cover. Leaves range from lance-shape to round, in all sizes. Leaf colors, patterns and textures include blue, green, variegated, smooth, and quilted. A flower spike appears in summer, with lilylike blooms of white, blue, or pale lavender.
**SOIL:** Not fussy about soil, but will do better if soil is rich.
**LIGHT:** Part shade
**HARDINESS:** Zone 3
**COMMENTS:** Hosta is one of the longest-lived perennials and one of the most care-free. It is rarely bothered by pests and will tolerate a variety of adverse growing conditions. To increase plants, dig and divide. Roots are tough; don't be afraid to pull them apart. Good choices include: *H. ventricosa, H. sieboldiana, H. undulata, H. plantaginea, H. decorata,* and *H. fortunei albomarginata.*

## IRIS
*Iris* species and hybrids

Of all the many types of iris grown, bearded iris is the most common. Plant height varies from only a few inches in the bulbous iris to the more common varieties growing 3 to 4 feet high. Flowers are solids or bicolors, in any color imaginable. Foliage is swordlike. If leaf ends dry out, cut them off with sharp shears for neatness.
**SOIL:** Average, well-drained, sandy soil, with a dry, alkaline consistency
**LIGHT:** Full sun
**HARDINESS:** Zone 4
**COMMENTS:** Bearded irises have many relatives that do well in the garden. Short, crested types, such as *I. cristata,* take a little more shade. The beardless iris likes a moister soil. Among the beardless are Japanese, Siberian, and water iris. Bulbous irises include Dutch iris and *I. reticulata.* Use them to line a border or mass them in a rock garden.

## PEONY
*Paeonia* hybrids

Garden dependability is synonymous with the peony. Long-lived plants form 2- to 4-foot-tall clumps and shrublike bunches. Flowers come in every shade except blue, but most are in tones of pink and red. Flower shapes are single; Japanese (single with large yellow centers); anemone (like the Japanese, with a powder-puff center); and double. A peony does best where winter temperatures drop to near or below zero.
**SOIL:** Slightly acidic; must have excellent drainage
**LIGHT:** Full sun
**HARDINESS:** Zone 5
**COMMENTS:** There are literally more peonies than you could ever grow. In choosing, look for your favorite color combinations. The blooms are all fragrant and fill the garden or home with a delicious scent. Since blooms do get heavy, they will usually need to be staked. Ants love peony buds, but generally do no harm.

### PHLOX
*Phlox* species

The phlox of the summer garden is a tall—to 6 feet—stately plant with clusters of flat, 5-petaled flowers appearing in mid- to late summer. Flower colors are in the white, red, pink, blue, and violet shades. Many have a contrasting eye. In contrast to this tall plant (*P. paniculata*), lower-growing phlox (*P. subulata* and *P. divaricata*) reach only 6 to 18 inches and are lovely in a rock garden. The former has pink or white flowers in the spring; the latter has blue flowers at the same time.

SOIL: Well-drained soil, kept cool with a mulch

LIGHT: Full sun

HARDINESS: Zone 5

COMMENTS: Phlox, an old-fashioned favorite, is subject to mildew. To prevent this, leave room between plants for air to circulate. Phlox should be grown from cuttings or divisions, because they revert to their original purple color when grown from seed.

### POPPY, ORIENTAL
*Papaver orientale*

The Oriental poppy is one of the top perennials that should be in every garden. Blooming in late spring or early summer, poppies have large, papery flowers of white, red, orange, or pink around a black center. The flowers can be single or double, and can be up to 6 inches across. Foliage is coarse and hairy; stems grow 2 to 4 feet high.

SOIL: Average, well drained. Plants will rot in a too-wet soil.

LIGHT: Full sun

HARDINESS: Zone 4

COMMENTS: Poppy foliage disappears after the plants bloom and reappears in early fall. Therefore, be prepared to surround the area with annuals so the flower bed will not be bare all summer. Poppies like cold winters and make excellent cut flowers.

### YARROW
*Achillea* species

Yarrow is a vigorous perennial used mostly in mixed beds, but sometimes useful in rock gardens or borders as well. Some varieties are as low-growing as 6 inches, but most reach 24 to 36 inches in height. Good for dried bouquets, flowers are golden yellow or reddish violet. Another species, known as sneezewort, has white flowers. Blooms are flat clusters of tiny flowers; the foliage is attractive and fernlike.

SOIL: Any soil—even the poorest—is acceptable. Yarrow is happy with dry soil. It even thrives in droughts.

LIGHT: Full sun

HARDINESS: Zone 3

COMMENTS: Yarrow can become weedy and overgrown, so give it an annual checkup and remove any unwanted plantlets. Flowers appear in June and again in September if cut back. Staking may be necessary. For beds or drying, try Coronation Gold, Moonshine, and Fire King.

# CARE AND MAINTENANCE

Perennials can be grown from seed, nursery-grown roots, or divisions of established plants. Although each perennial has its own care requirements, follow these general tips to ensure success in the border.

## SOIL PREPARATION

■ Because a perennial grows in the same spot for many years, preparing soil in the bed is the first important step toward getting a plant of top-notch quality. As early in the spring as the ground can be worked, turn the soil the full depth of the spade. Mix in a generous amount of organic matter and a fertilizer rich in phosphorus, such as bonemeal or superphosphate. Rake the ground level.

## HOW TO PLANT

■ Dig holes big enough to handle the large roots of many perennials. Set plants at the same level they grew before and tamp them carefully into place without breaking the roots. After planting, mark the location of the new plants and water well. Space plants according to the distances recommended in the chart on page 26; spacing should accommodate their size at maturity and allow good air circulation. Watering is particularly important with new plants until they become well established.

## POST-PLANTING CARE

■ In early spring, apply an all-purpose fertilizer, such as 5-10-5, and water in lightly. For an extra boost during the blooming season, apply water-soluble plant food to the foliage and soil.

After the soil has warmed up, apply a summer mulch to keep the soil cool and moist and to keep weeds down.

Tall, top-heavy perennials, such as hollyhock (*above*), delphinium, and foxglove, often fall over and need help to stay upright. In early spring, set stakes in the soil and tie the stems as they grow.

To keep perennials blooming, remove flowers as soon as they fade. Known as deadheading, this procedure forces fresh growth and encourages new bud formation.

Other perennials, such as black-eyed susan (*above*) and baby's-breath, have bushy plants on wiry stems that arch over. Set several stakes around the clump and hold together with twine.

## WINTER PROTECTION

■ After the first killing frost in the fall, cut and remove all dead stalks and trim stems to within an inch or two of the ground. Next, apply a winter mulch of leaves or straw. If rainfall has been light during summer and fall months, deeply water your perennials.

Oriental poppies and Madonna lilies send up growth in the fall that needs extra care. A pot placed over the foliage will provide good protection, or build a tent over the plant with two wire hoops covered with heavy cloth or paper.

## DIVIDING

■ Perennials will bloom more vigorously if they're divided every few years. A plant needs dividing when it shows weak or dying center growth, crowds out neighboring plants, or produces less-than-spectacular blooms.

Most plants should be divided in early spring, as soon as new growth appears. Others—including iris, lily, and Oriental poppy—do better if you divide them in late summer or fall. Follow the same steps for transplanting as you would for setting in new plants.

As soon as frost has blackened the tops of perennials, cut and remove dead stalks, leaving just an inch or two so you can tell in the spring where the plants are.

Any garden can use a well-designed cold frame. The cold frame *above* has a slanted top and a back several inches higher than the front. The removable top is made of inexpensive plastic.

Use cold frames for hardening off new seedlings in spring, and overwintering (providing a warmer winter home for plants) summer seedlings and tender perennials dug before fall frost.

After you remove dead foliage and other debris, cover beds with a winter mulch of evergreen boughs, leaves, or straw in cold climates. Hold mulch in place by anchoring chicken wire over it.

# BULBS IN THE LANDSCAPE

Nothing says "spring" better than a magnificent display of blooms that have grown from bulbs, especially when that display is tastefully integrated into your home's landscape. Long before any color bursts from other plants, shoots from such early-blooming bulbs as winter aconite (eranthis) and snowdrop (galanthus) poke their heads through the thawing soil. Many will blossom even when snow clings to the ground.

A little later, while days are still bleak and trees and shrubs still bare, crocus, Grecian windflower (anemone), Siberian squill (scilla), glory-of-the-snow (chionodoxa), and puschkinia begin to show off their blossoms. Because these bulbs bloom before grass starts to grow, they can be naturalized in the lawn, like the crocus, anemone, and scilla *below*.

Late spring heralds a mixed chorus of blooms from such bulbs as tulip, hyacinth, daffodil, snowflake (leucojum), fritillaria, oxalis, and allium. Planted en masse, these larger bulbs—such as the tulips and hyacinths at *right*—help fill the color void between spring's flowering trees and shrubs and summer's annuals and perennials.

Plant bulbs where you and passersby can most enjoy them. Along with growing in the lawn, these spring charmers do well around the base of trees near the house, or in small clumps at the front door. Squeeze them into the corner of a rock garden or use them as a border in front of a foundation planting. For continuous and everchanging color, select different types of flowers with complementary heights and col-

# BULBS IN THE LANDSCAPE

Steep slopes and rock walls can be smothered with spring color by using bulbs as a season starter. To turn a barren hillside into a spring-to-fall kaleidoscope of bright color, mix bulbs with perennials and annuals between shrubs and other permanent features. At *right,* tulips, hyacinths, and daffodils combine with candytuft, creeping phlox, and pansies for a dazzling look.

Bulbs also can be nestled between stones in rock gardens to help hold the soil in place. Clumps of low-growing spring-blooming bulbs—such as glory-of-the-snow, puschkinia, Siberian squill, dwarf tulip, and dwarf narcissus—work best. Small shrubs and perennials will complete the attractive picture.

Your overall garden design will be more stunning if you harmonize bulbs with existing trees and shrubs. In front of forsythia (*right*), early tulips and daffodils form an enchanting silhouette, framed by a border of pansies. Blooming at the same time, hyacinths can blanket the ground under magnolias or in front of p.j.m. rhododendrons.

Grape hyacinths, which bloom a little later, add a complementary blue contrast to the pinks of flowering crabapple, cherry, and peach. Dutch iris and wood hyacinth team up beautifully with late-blooming azaleas, Scotch broom, and dogwood. The giant allium will add an interesting accent to early perennials such as iris and peonies.

Spring-blooming bulbs can dress up those awkward, hard-to-plant areas in your yard. The two drab driveways at *left* were brilliantly separated with a narrow bed of daffodils and tulips. As those blossoms fade, summer annuals and fall mums continue the color show. Crocus, snowdrops, and winter aconite can be added for even earlier bloom.

Under trees, create a natural woodland effect with grape hyacinths, daffodils, galanthus, or scilla. Because they'll bloom before the trees leaf out, these bulbs will get plenty of sunlight for maximum blooming power.

Colors will set the mood in your bulb garden. Bright reds, yellows, and oranges are warm and exciting; blue, white, and lavender are more cooling and soothing to the eye.

A drift of bulbs near a kitchen or family room window will bring the beauty of springtime bloom indoors. At *left,* tulips and daffodils combine with pansies to make a vivid sight under a picture window. This raised bed also improves drainage in a heavy soil. To fill the rooms of your home with sweet fragrances, plant hyacinths, daffodils, or lilies in flower beds near windows that can be opened.

Consider the view from near and far when designing your spring bulb borders. Tiny early-flowering specimens, such as snowdrops, species crocus, winter aconite, and *Iris reticulata,* should be set near doors and driveways where they will be noticed.

# BULB PLANTING

You get what you pay for when you buy bulbs. For superior flowers, choose top-quality bulbs. Look for large, firm bulbs with no visible dents, scars, or bruises. If you skimp by selecting small bulbs, you may be disappointed with poor performance and small flowers.

## HOW TO PLAN A BORDER

■ A garden plan will help you achieve the desired effect. Sketch your garden, indicating the position of trees, shrubs, and other permanent features. Select bulbs for each location, based on sunlight, existing and desired color, and continuity of bloom times. Consider height also; ground-hugging scilla, for example, will not look as good in front of large trees as stately tulips will.

Decide before planting whether you want a formal or an informal look for your bulb garden. The style of your home and the rest of the garden may determine this for you. The formal garden, with its symmetrical borders, should be planted with a formal flower, such as tulips and hyacinths. It also should have a limited number of colors; one color is best. Informal beds, which are more natural in appearance, should have bulbs planted in drifts of color for more of a rainbow effect.

## WHEN TO PLANT

■ Plant hardy bulbs in the fall, before frost hardens the ground. If you can't plant your bulbs immediately, store them in a dark, dry, cool—but not freezing—place to keep them from sprouting or shriveling. To spread out the work, plant the smaller, earlier-flowering bulbs first and do the larger bulbs last. Bulbs can be planted with a special bulb planter or a narrow trowel.

## WHERE TO PLANT

■ Bulbs prefer full sun or light shade. The best planting site is an area that gets light shade during the warmest part of the day. Afternoon shade can prolong the lives of the flowers and help retain their deep colors. Heavy shade from structures or a dense grove of trees, however, will weaken bulbs and cause a less-than-spectacular blossom display the following spring. Planted under deciduous trees, spring-blooming bulbs will benefit from filtered sunlight before the trees leaf out.

## HOW TO PLANT

■ Planted formally or informally, bulbs will show off their blooms better when they're planted in a clump rather than individually lined up or scattered. For the most spectacular display, mass at least 20 bulbs of the same variety and color. In a mixed border, space bulbs (at least 5 to a group) among perennials that will bloom later. The perennials will hide ripening bulb foliage.

For a solid color effect, space tulips and other big bulbs 5 or 6 inches apart; smaller bulbs can be placed closer together. Plant large bulbs—such as tulip and daffodil—8 inches deep, and smaller ones—such as crocus—only 4 inches deep. A good rule of thumb is that planting depth should equal three times the diameter of the bulb.

Bulbs require a soil that has good drainage. Heavy, compact soil prevents good root growth; waterlogged soil will make the bulbs rot. To improve drainage before you plant, work a generous amount of well-rotted compost or manure into the soil.

**1** Good soil preparation is key to a successful bulb garden. Because bulb roots reach deep, you'll need to spade and prepare the bed to a depth of 12 inches. Rake to even the surface.

**2** If you want your bulb plantings to look natural, arrange them in an informal design. Toss bulbs randomly, then plant them where they fall. (You may have to adjust them slightly to maintain spacing.)

**3** Although bulbs contain their first season's food supply, fertilizing fosters future growth. To encourage root growth, add phosphorus-rich bonemeal to the bottom of each planting hole.

**4** If squirrels, chipmunks, or other small animals are a problem in your area and threaten to make dinner of your bulbs, sink bulbs in a wire basket, or spread chicken wire over the planting.

**5** When planting a mass of bulbs, dig a large planting hole, rather than make many individual holes. Make the hole 9 to 12 inches deep, then refill it with loose soil until the depth is correct for your bulbs.

**6** After planting, cover with soil, water well, and mulch with leaves. Label the bed so you know where the bulbs are planted. In spring, remove leaves as soon as bulb foliage begins to appear.

# GALLERY OF BULBS

## ALLIUM
*Allium* species

If you have ever seen the blooms of the onion and the garlic, you might recognize their relation to the allium. The globe flower shape is easily identified, even in allium's varied shapes and colors. *A. giganteum*—tallest of the group—has flower stalks 3 to 5 feet tall over a base of foliage. Flowers are purple and appear in early summer. *A. moly* is about 12 inches tall with golden yellow flowers in midsummer. Drumstick allium (*A. sphaerocephalum*) produces giant red blooms on 2-foot-tall stalks. *A. karataviense* is silvery pink in late spring.
**SOIL:** Rich, well drained
**LIGHT:** Full sun
**PLANTING DEPTH:** Small, 5 inches; Large, 8 inches
**PLANTING DISTANCE:** Small, 4 inches; Large, 12 inches
**COMMENTS:** Water well during the growing season. Fertilize when foliage starts to appear.

## ANEMONE (Grecian windflower)
*Anemone blanda*

The Grecian windflower is a small, daisylike flower in shades of blue, pink, or white that blooms in early to mid-spring. Stunning when massed, blooms are about 2 to 3 inches across with a bright yellow center. Foliage is starlike and grows close to the ground.
**SOIL:** Fast draining
**LIGHT:** Full sun or light shade
**PLANTING DEPTH:** 4 inches
**PLANTING DISTANCE:** 4 to 6 inches
**COMMENTS:** Anemones are grown from tubers, but react like plants grown from true bulbs. They are not winter-hardy north of Zone 6. In Zone 6 and north, the relatives of the Grecian windflower such as anemone De Caen and anemone St. Brigid are not hardy and must be dug every fall and replanted every spring. These two anemones have large, poppylike flowers in bright shades of red, blue, violet, or purple.

## *Chionodoxa luciliae*
Glory-of-the-snow

These little bulbs are among the first to pop their heads out of the ground in early spring, blooming about the same time as the crocus. Flowers are mostly blue, but a few are white or pink. The six-petaled, starlike flowers have a light center. Spikes of blooms are 4 to 5 inches high, growing from the center of straplike leaves. Chionodoxa is one of the easiest bulbs to grow. It never requires dividing. Extremely hardy, it will thrive in cold climates.
**SOIL:** Average to dry soil
**LIGHT:** Full sun or part shade
**PLANTING DEPTH:** 4 inches
**PLANTING DISTANCE:** 3 inches
**COMMENTS:** The glory-of-the-snow should be left undisturbed after blooming; the seeds scatter easily and germinate readily, quickly producing large colonies of plants. An excellent bulb for naturalizing.

## CROCUS
*Crocus* species and hybrids

The most popular of all the little bulbs, crocuses are available in a host of breathtaking colors and bicolors. The species crocus are smaller, earlier to bloom, and less spectacular. Their multicolored flowers have a purple stripe. They open in the sunshine and close in the afternoon. The hybrid crocus are much larger and more outstanding, with blooms of white, lavender, purple, or yellow. Narrow, long foliage is deep green, often with a stripe.

SOIL: Rich, well-drained soil
LIGHT: Full sun or part shade
PLANTING DEPTH: 4 inches
PLANTING DISTANCE: 3 inches
COMMENTS: Mass crocuses around the bases of trees and shrubs, or along the edge of a winding garden path. These pint-size, ground-hugging charmers don't need to be dug, divided or replanted. Clumps will spread by seeds; new plants, however, may not bloom for several years.

## DAFFODILS
*Narcissus* species and hybrids

Narcissus is the botanical name of the whole family, but the narcissus is also a short-cupped member of the family. Daffodil is the common name for the tribe, but also refers to those flowers with long trumpets. The golden blooms of the daffodil are one of the most refreshing sights in mid-spring. Daffodils and jonquils bloom atop stems that range from 6 to 12 inches high in a variety of flower shapes. The flowers are white, yellow, or a combination of both with a few varieties that come close to being pink. Many are fragrant.

SOIL: Well-drained, rich soil
LIGHT: Full sun to part shade
PLANTING DEPTH: 8 inches
PLANTING DISTANCE: 6 to 12 inches, depending on the variety
COMMENTS: Daffodils are excellent bulbs for naturalizing, but since their foliage hangs on until early summer, be sure to put them in a place where they can be left undisturbed.

## *Eranthis hyemalis*
### Winter aconite

The winter aconite is an early-to-bloom plant, often appearing when snow still covers the ground. Dainty, golden yellow, 2-inch flowers have a waxy consistency. The six-petaled, sweetly fragrant blooms resemble buttercups and appear on stems barely taller than a mushroom. The shiny, thick, deep green foliage rays out from underneath the flower in a starlike pattern.

SOIL: Rich, moist, well-drained soil
LIGHT: Full sun or part shade
PLANTING DEPTH: 4 inches
PLANTING DISTANCE: 3 to 4 inches
COMMENTS: Winter aconite grows from a tuber with no apparent top or bottom. Plant it in late summer as soon as you receive it, after soaking it in water or moist sand overnight to restore lost moisture. If winter aconite dries out, it will not survive.

# GALLERY OF BULBS

### FRITILLARIA
*Fritillaria* species

This purple and white checkered flower droops from thin stems like a Tiffany lamp. The six petals also look like an upside-down tulip. Petals, about 2 inches long, appear in mid-spring on stems approximately 6 to 12 inches high. The thin, grasslike leaves are about the same length as the flower stem.

SOIL: Average
LIGHT: Full sun to part shade
PLANTING DEPTH: 4 inches;
*F. imperialis*, 8 inches
PLANTING DISTANCE: 5 inches
COMMENTS: The fritillaria should be thought of as a unique addition to the garden. It is not a plant for massing, but it is one to locate close to where you and passersby can appreciate it. A relative of fritillaria is the Crown Imperial (*F. imperialis*), which grows 4 feet high and is topped with a hanging orange flower with leaves atop.

### GALANTHUS (snowdrops)
*Galanthus nivalis*

Another gem among the early blooming bulbs are snowdrops, which often appear while snow still rests on the ground. Three-part flowers drop from a thin stem about 4 to 6 inches tall. The white flowers have waxy green tips on the inner surfaces that are revealed as the petals open in the sunlight. Greenish gray, grasslike foliage is about the same height as the flower stems.

SOIL: Average
LIGHT: Full sun or part shade
PLANTING DEPTH: 4 inches
PLANTING DISTANCE: 2 inches
COMMENTS: Snowdrops are a very care-free plant, perfectly suited for a woodland area where their white flowers stand out against the dark soil and leaves. They look their best if planted in colonies or clumps and left to naturalize. Since they are not as long-lived as other bulbs, you may need to replace them more often.

### HYACINTH
*Hyacinthus* hybrids

Few things are more delightful than the sweet scent of hyacinths in mid-spring. The rounded clusters of small, star-shaped flowers are as pretty to look at as they are fragrant. Available in shades of red, white, pink, blue, purple, or yellow, the 6- to 8-inch flowers grow from the center of straplike leaves.

SOIL: Rich, well-drained soil
LIGHT: Full sun to light shade
PLANTING DEPTH: 8 inches
PLANTING DISTANCE: 6 inches
COMMENTS: To make the most of their fragrance, plant hyacinths near a window, breakfast nook, or other areas where you can catch their scent in a breeze. Blooms also can be cut and used indoors to fill an entire room with a natural air freshener. Unfortunately, hyacinths lose some of their compactness after a few years, and become loose, thin clusters. When this occurs, replace them.

## LEUCOJUM
*Leucojum aestivum*

Ring in the month of May with an enchanting display of leucojum. Also called summer snowflake, leucojum's white, bell-shape flowers are attractively edged in green. The plants grow about 15 inches tall and the blooms make long-lasting cut flowers. They are in bloom at the same time as lily-of-the-valley and look good as companions.

**SOIL:** Average
**LIGHT:** Part shade
**PLANTING DEPTH:** 4 inches
**PLANTING DISTANCE:** 4 inches
**COMMENTS:** Once planted, summer snowflake needs little care. They rarely need dividing, and the foliage disappears quickly after blooming, letting you replace them with annuals.

## STAR-OF-BETHLEHEM
*Ornithogalum umbellatum*

If you have a spot in the garden where absolutely nothing will grow, don't despair. Star-of-Bethlehem will thrive even under the most adverse conditions. It fills in the mid-spring garden with a carpet of white, six-petaled, star-shape flowers that bloom in clusters on stems about 6 inches high. Each flower is about ½ to 1 inch across, with a thin green stripe on the outside of each petal. Foliage on the star-of-Bethlehem is very dense and grassy.

**SOIL:** Average to poor
**LIGHT:** Full sun to part shade
**PLANTING DEPTH:** 4 inches
**PLANTING DISTANCE:** 3 to 4 inches
**COMMENTS:** Another of star-of-Bethlehem's attributes is its long-lasting qualities as a cut flower. The contrast between the white flowers and the black center with yellow stamens is most attractive.

## TULIP
*Tulipa* species and hybrids

Think of tulips and you think of a tall, stately, formal look. Tulips are the spring favorite for massed beds of color, including red, white, blue, purple, yellow, pink, coral, and black. Hardly any other flower has the tulip's diversity of color and form. Flowers range from the classic, six-petaled cottage or Darwin tulips, to the fringed parrot, pointed lily, and starburst miniature types. Many hybrids grow atop a stem up to 30 inches tall, while the species tulips tend to be lower growing.

**SOIL:** Rich, fast-draining soil
**LIGHT:** Full sun
**PLANTING DEPTH:** Species, 4 inches; all others, 8 inches
**PLANTING DISTANCE:** 4 to 6 inches
**COMMENTS:** For best effect, plant tulips in a mass of one color or variety, not in a single row of mixed color. Plant several varieties and you'll have blooms for up to six weeks.

# CARE AND MAINTENANCE

Even if you've properly prepared your bulb bed at planting time, you'll need to tend to your bulbs throughout the season to get maximum results.

### FERTILIZING
■ Bulbs contain their first season's food supply, but you'll need to add fertilizer each year to keep the bulbs healthy and flowering at their best. Each spring, as soon as the leaves begin to emerge, sprinkle a balanced fertilizer on the ground and water it in well. For maximum results, feed again just prior to blooming and once more as the foliage starts to yellow.

### WATERING
■ Proper flowering and growth also depend on a sufficient amount of moisture reaching the root zone. If you have a rainless spring, you'll have to provide supplementary water. During such dry spells, water your bulbs deeply and regularly after shoots appear.

### MULCHING
■ Mulching bulb beds in the fall insulates the soil to prevent extreme temperature fluctuations during the winter. An unprotected bed is prone to alternate freezing and thawing, which can heave bulbs out of their resting places. Use an organic mulch such as leaves, compost, wood chips, or pine needles.

### PEST CONTROL
■ Bulbs are subject to few insects or diseases. If a bulb shows signs of disease, such as misshapen or discolored flowers, lift and destroy the entire plant to prevent the problem from spreading.

Field mice, squirrels, and chipmunks like to dig up and eat bulbs. Nothing is completely effective in keeping rodents away, but a few techniques help. (See wire basket, photo 4 on page 37.) To reduce the threat from animals, plant bulbs away from walls or house foundations where rodents make runs. Before planting bulbs, clean beds of all garden refuse to prevent mice from setting up permanent housekeeping.

Once bulbs are up and growing, squirrels often will make a feast of foliage and flowers. To discourage them, dust the leaves with thiram (which has an odor that rodents do not like) or dried blood; reapply after every rainfall. You also can use commercial repellents, or make your own by soaking felt strips with creosote or Tabasco sauce and hanging them near the garden.

**When tulips** (*above*), **daffodils, and hyacinths have finished blooming, cut off seed heads to direct energy to the bulbs. Smaller bulbs can be left to go to seed. The seeds will scatter and multiply.**

**Where neatness counts in a formal flower border, braid the yellowing foliage on large bulbs, or twirl the leaves into a circle until they ripen. In informal gardens, leave foliage undisturbed.**

**When danger of frost has passed, annuals—such as the petunias** *above*—**can be set into the garden around the bulb plants. Avoid damaging the bulbs when digging.**

## AFTER-BLOOM CARE

■ Bulbs get nourishment for the following spring's display from the current season's foliage. To let the leaves ripen naturally, avoid cutting or mowing the foliage until it turns brown and pulls easily away from the plant.

The most successful gardens provide continuous color from spring's first snowdrop to autumn's last chrysanthemum. In a mixed border, perennials will take over about the time bulbs finish blooming. If unsightly bulb foliage still shows, you can sow seeds of annual flowers, such as zinnias and marigolds, in the open areas between the clumps. Bulbs also are useful in rose beds; rose foliage emerges after the bulbs have passed their peak.

Some bulbs, such as tulip and hyacinth, are never as vigorous the second season. Many gardeners dig up and discard these bulbs after they bloom, then replant in the fall. If time and your budget don't allow you to replace your tulip and hyacinth bulbs each year, the bulbs will continue to produce lovely blossoms for a few more years.

Bulbs that are used for only one flowering season may be planted in areas not normally well suited for perennial treatment. Drifts of tulips, for example, can be planted even in heavily shaded areas. Extensive soil preparation and fertilizing are not necessary.

Many of the smaller bulbs, such as scilla, chionodoxa, and puschkinia, will spread with each bloom period, and can be left in place after they bloom. If these bulbs are naturalized in your lawn, avoid mowing the grass until the bulb foliage has ripened.

New bulbs that form at the sides of a daffodil bulb can be carefully pulled off and replanted. Don't expect too much from them the first year, but in time, they'll be as good as the originals.

## DIVIDING

■ Daffodils and crocuses should be dug up and divided every few years, when the clumps get overcrowded and the quantity and size of blooms decline. Spring is the best time to divide, right after the foliage turns yellow. Bulbs are easier to locate in the spring because you can still see the leaves. In the fall, you risk damaging bulbs if you randomly dig for them.

When moving bulbs, dig them carefully to avoid bruising or cutting them, or disturbing their roots. Replant them immediately, following the method on page 37 for planting new bulbs in the fall. Leave the foliage in place after planting, and let it mature as though the bulb had not been moved.

# FORCING BULBS

Springtime comes early when you force bulbs into bloom indoors. When winter winds howl outdoors, tulips, hyacinths, daffodils, and crocuses (*below, right*) will bring bright colors, lovely scents, and the cheer of fresh flowers into your home. Two other good choices for forcing are paperwhite narcissus and amaryllis. Potted in fall, all of these bulbs will bloom in time for the holidays.

Depending on the amount of sunlight and the temperature, it takes 12 to 14 weeks to force a bulb into bloom. (Paperwhites and amaryllis will bloom in 4 to 8 weeks.) For continuous color all winter, plant a pot each week.

### HOW TO PLANT
■ Create an indoor bulb garden by massing one or more types. A 6-inch container will accommodate six tulips;

three daffodils or hyacinths; or 15 crocus, grape hyacinths, or small iris.

Pots should be at least twice as deep as the bulbs to allow for proper root growth. Set the flat edge of tulip bulbs at the outside of the container. Label each pot, and record planting and bloom dates for reference next year.

### BEFORE-BLOOM CARE
■ After you plant and water the bulbs, give them an artificial winter by keeping them in a cold location (where temperatures stay above freezing, ideally between 35 and 45 degrees Fahrenheit) for 12 to 14 weeks. You can use a refrigerator, an unheated garage or porch, a cool basement, a cold frame, or a trench outdoors. If you use a trench, dig it 6 inches deeper than the largest pot and line the bottom with gravel for drainage. Place pots in the trench, cover with soil, and apply a 3- to 4-inch layer of mulch to prevent the soil from freezing. Water only to keep the soil in the pots from drying out.

Fragrance and color are two benefits you'll get from bulbs. Clustered in a basket, small pots with *Scilla campanulata* and *Iris reticulata* (*above*) make a delightful miniature indoor garden.

To avoid the 12- to 14-week cooling period, you can buy precooled bulbs and start them growing right away. Another way to grow bulbs is to set them in a bowl filled with water so the bottom of the bulb just touches the water. Treat them as you would the precooled bulbs planted in soil.

Bring the pots indoors when shoots are 2 to 3 inches tall. For the first ten days, keep the pots in indirect sun at a temperature of 55 to 60 degrees Fahrenheit. After that, you can move them to a sunny spot, but keep them away from heat and drafts. To provide adequate humidity, set the pots on pebbles in trays of water. Within 3 to 4 weeks, the flowers will appear, transforming your winter-weary home into springtime. Prolong blooming by keeping the pots as cool as possible. In a greenhouse, keep them out of direct sun.

## AFTER-BLOOM CARE

■ After the flowers fade, move pots to a cool, sunny spot so leaves can naturally ripen while bulbs gain strength for new growth. Most bulbs forced indoors cannot be forced again, but can be planted outdoors. Paperwhite narcissus and amaryllis are two exceptions to this rule. Discard paperwhite bulbs after they bloom; amaryllis can be repotted the following year for more blooms.

1 Select a container that is at least twice as tall as your bulbs. Fill the pot ¾ full with a lightweight potting soil. Place bulbs a pencil-width apart on top of the soil, then gently press them into the soil.

2 A 10- to 12-inch pot will hold 16 paperwhite narcissus bulbs. The growing tip or nose of the bulbs should be even with the top of the pot. Water thoroughly, then keep soil evenly moist.

3 Add more soil around the bulbs. Place pot in a cold area where temperatures stay above freezing. When stems are 2 to 3 inches tall, move pot to a bright window away from direct sunlight.

45

# CONSIDER YOUR CLIMATE

The climatic conditions in your area are a mixture of different weather patterns: sun, snow, rain, wind, and humidity. A good gardener is aware of all of the variations in temperature and conditions in his or her own garden, from how much rainfall it receives each year to the high and low temperatures of a typical growing season.

The zone map at *right* gives an approximate range of minimum temperatures across the country. Most plants are rated by these zones for conditions where they grow best.

However, zone boundary lines are not absolute. You can obtain the general information for your area from your state agricultural school or your county extension agent.

Be sure to study the microclimates that characterize your own plot of ground. Land on the south side of your house is bound to be warmer than a constantly shaded area exposed to cold, northwest winds. Being aware of the variations in your garden will help you choose the best plant for the prevailing conditions and avoid disappointment.

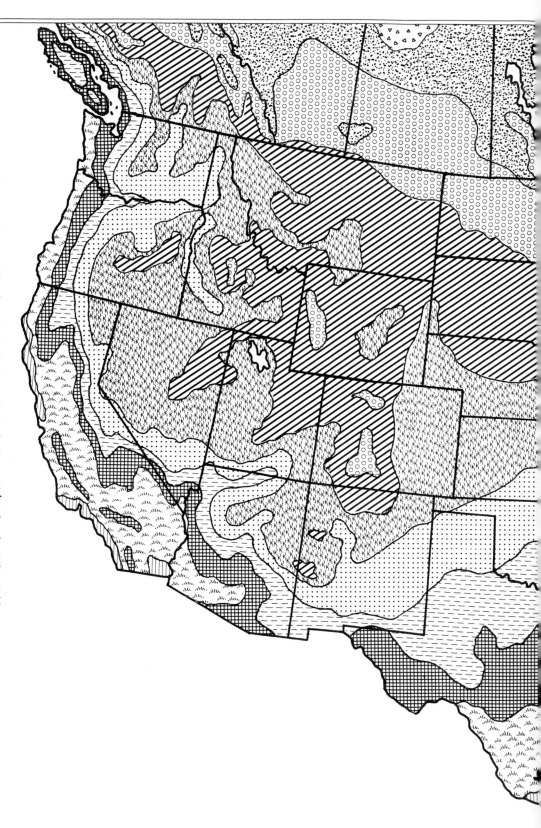

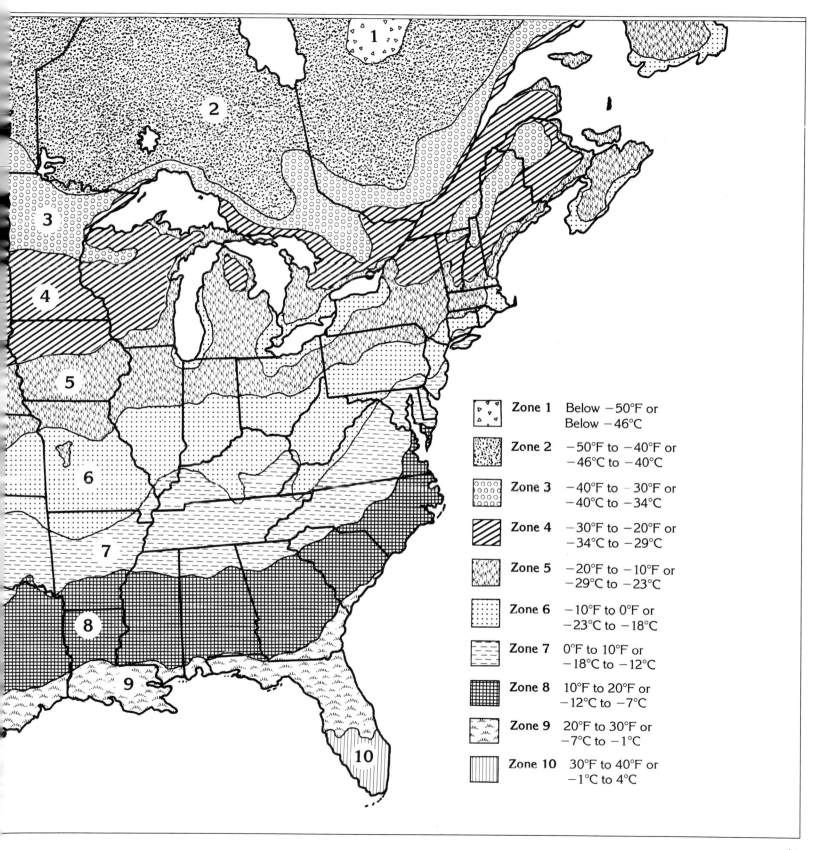

| | Zone 1 | Below −50°F or Below −46°C |
| --- | --- | --- |
| | Zone 2 | −50°F to −40°F or −46°C to −40°C |
| | Zone 3 | −40°F to −30°F or −40°C to −34°C |
| | Zone 4 | −30°F to −20°F or −34°C to −29°C |
| | Zone 5 | −20°F to −10°F or −29°C to −23°C |
| | Zone 6 | −10°F to 0°F or −23°C to −18°C |
| | Zone 7 | 0°F to 10°F or −18°C to −12°C |
| | Zone 8 | 10°F to 20°F or −12°C to −7°C |
| | Zone 9 | 20°F to 30°F or −7°C to −1°C |
| | Zone 10 | 30°F to 40°F or −1°C to 4°C |

# INDEX

## A–D

Aconite, winter, 39
Allium, 38
Anemone, 38
  naturalized, 32
Annuals, 4–17
  around bulb plants, 42
  care and maintenance of,
    16–17
  for climate, 6, 17
  in containers, 7, 14–15
  in landscape, 4–7
  with perennials, 18–19, 22
  for shaded area, 7
  sizes and shapes of, 6
  soil for, 6, 8, 10–11
  spacing guidelines for, 10
  starting from cuttings, 17
  starting from seeds:
    indoors, 8
    outdoors, 10–11
  starting from transplants, 12
Borders:
  annual, 4
  bulb, planning, 36
  perennial:
    examples, 18, 20, 21
    planning, 22–23
Bulbs, 32–45
  care of, 42–43
  forcing, 44–45
  gallery of 38–41
  in landscape, 32–35
  light requirements of, 36
    by species, 38–41
  planting, 36–37
    depth and spacing,
      36, 38–41
    indoors, 44–45
Candytuft, 26
Care and maintenance:
  of annuals, 16–17
    in containers, 14
  of bulbs, 42–43
    forced, 44–45
  of perennials, 30–31

Chionodoxa, 38
Chrysanthemum, 26
Cold frame for perennials, 31
Coleus cuttings rooting, 17
Container plants:
  annuals, 7, 14–15
  forced bulbs, 44–45
Coreopsis, 27
Crocus, 39
  dividing, 43
  forced, 44–45
  naturalized, 32
Cutting:
  annuals, 16, 17
  bulb seed heads, 42
  perennials, 30, 31
Cuttings from annuals,
  rooting, 17
Daffodil, 39
  dividing, 43
  forced, 44–45
  in landscape, 34–35
Daylily, 27
Deadheading:
  annuals, 16
  perennials, 30
Delphinium, 27
Dividing:
  bulbs, 43
  perennials, 31

## E–O

Eranthis, 39
Feeding with fertilizer:
  annuals, 16
  bulbs, 37, 42
  perennials, 30
Forcing of bulbs, 44–45
Fritillaria, 40
Funkia, 28
Galanthus, 40
Glory-of-the-snow, 38
Grecian windflower, 38
Hemerocallis (daylily), 27
Hollyhock, staking, 30
Hosta, 28
Hyacinth, 40
  forced, 44–45
  in landscape, 32–34
  in second season, 43

Impatiens, 7
Iris, 28
  potted, 44
Leucojum, 41
Lily family:
  daylily, 27
  plantain lily, 28
Mulch:
  for annuals, 16
  winter:
    for bulbs, 37, 42
    for perennials, 31
Narcissus:
  daffodil, 39
    dividing, 43
    forced, 44–45
    in landscape, 34–35
  paperwhite, forcing, 45
Oriental poppy, 29

## P–Z

Pansies:
  with bulbs in landscape,
    34–35
  as cool-weather plant, 17
Paperwhite narcissus,
  forcing, 45
Peony, 28
Perennials, 18–31
  borders:
    examples, 18, 20, 21
    planning, 22–23
  care and maintenance of,
    30–31
  colors for, 21, 22
    by species, 24–29
  gallery of, 26–29
  in landscape, 18–21
  light requirements of:
    shade-loving, 21
    by species, 26–29
    sun–loving, 22
  planting, 30
Pest control:
  for annuals, 16
  for bulbs, 37, 42
Petunia:
  around bulb plants, 42
  cutting back, 16, 17
Phlox, 29

Plantain lily, 28
Potted plants:
  annuals, 7, 14–15
  forced bulbs, 44–45
Rodent control for bulbs,
  37, 42
Rooting of cuttings from
  annuals, 17
Scilla:
  naturalized, 32
  potted, 44
Seedlings, annual:
  indoor-started, 8
  thinning, 11
Seeds, starting annuals from:
  indoors, 8
  outdoors, 10–11
Snowdrop, 40
Snowflake (leucojum), 41
Soil:
  for annuals, 6
    potting media, 8
    preparation of, 10–11
  for bulbs, 36, 37
    requirements by species,
      38–41
  for perennials, 23, 30
    requirements by species,
      26–29
Star-of-Bethlehem, 41
Summer snowflake
  (leucojum), 41
Tickseed, 27
Transplanting of annuals:
  bedding plants, 12
  seedlings, 8
Tulip, 41
  after first season, 43
  forced, 44–45
  in landscape, 32–35
  seed heads, cutting off, 42
Windflower, Grecian, 38
Winter aconite, 39
Yarrow, 29
Zones, climate, map of, 46–47